Breakthrough Marketing With A Guaranteed Difference

Getting Your Toronto Condo SOLD Fast For The Best Price

By **Thomas Cook**

Real estate sales representative @ RE/MAX since 1983

Copyright © 2018 Thomas Cook
All rights reserved.
ISBN-10: 1546787577
ISBN-13: 978-1546787570

ABOUT THE AUTHOR

Let's start off by giving you a little background about where I'm coming from in terms of experience and knowledge. I've been in the real estate industry since 1980. While originally with Royal LePage, I switched to RE/MAX Hallmark in 1983, where I have been ever since.

Along with helping literally thousands of people to buy and sell their homes, over the years I've been involved in a number of other real estate related activities as well. For example, through the '80s I had a property management company and at times managed up to 350 single-family homes, duplexes, triplexes, condos, and small four- and eight-unit buildings, mainly for investors but often for people who were out of the city on a job transfer and wanted to maintain their existing residence.

That has provided some great insight into such things as tenant related issues, understanding of the Tenant Protection Act, and knowledge on how to design a really good rental application and a comprehensive lease. I find those things help today with clients who are interested in buying something that has a rental component to it — maybe the traditional basement rental apartment where the owner lives upstairs, or more likely today a downtown Toronto condominium suite.

I've renovated about twenty-five homes in Toronto, as well as building a triplex from the ground up in Riverdale. In 2008, I built a cottage in the Kawarthas that started with an uncleared lot. These experiences certainly provided some great insights into working with contractors, dealing with City Hall for building permits, and even on occasion going to the Committee of Adjustment or the OMB (Ontario Municipal Board) when obtaining a permit requires applying for a variance.

I find these experiences help with clients who might be interested in buying something that needs renovation or fix up work.

I can certainly offer advice and answer those kinds of questions for my clients — and many more.

For several years, I also had a mortgage company, which provided a lot of insight into mortgage financing and learning how to package the buyer's mortgage application to get clients the best possible rate and terms.

During my 38+ year career, my Team and I have helped over 2500 buyers and sellers reach their real estate goals. This achievement has earned me one of the highest RE/MAX sales production awards… the Circle Of Legends.

TORONTO'S REAL ESTATE TEAM MISSION STATEMENT

Our goal is to give you such an exceptional home selling or buying experience that you will feel compelled to tell all your friends and family about us.

We use our time each and every day to its fullest potential, always remembering that our clients pay us to work diligently to get their home sold, or find their next home for purchase.

We strive to deliver more value to you than you expect to receive and to provide uncompromising service based on integrity, fairness, knowledge, professionalism and enthusiasm.

Once your real estate transaction has been completed, we'd be honoured if you were to refer our services to everyone you know so they could share the same excellent experience you enjoyed.

LOTS OF WAYS TO GET IN TOUCH...

Thomas Cook
Real Estate Sales Representative @ RE/MAX Hallmark Realty Ltd Brokerage

Mobile-Text | 647-962-1650
Office | 416-465-7850

Web | LivingInToronto.com
Email | Thomas@LivingInToronto.com

Author of '**Inside Tips To Getting The Best Price**' designed specifically for Toronto condominium owners and sellers.

Author | Ultimate Toronto Home Buyer's Guide (THE 'Bible' for TO buyers)
Author | Toronto Home Buyer's Financing Guide
Author | Free Government Money Report (For 1st-time buyers)
Author | Insider Tips For Getting The Best Price (For condo sellers)
Author | Guide To Attracting The Best Tenants
Author | Best Capital Gains Tax Advice (Excellent investor advice)
Author | Guide To Downtown Toronto Condo Prices
Author | Insider Advice For House Sellers (For house sellers)

Experience || Thousands of homes sold since 1980
Professional Designations || ABR, SRES
Awards || RE/MAX's 2ND highest award - Circle Of Legends
Charity Support || Over $117,500 contributed to the Toronto Sick Kids Hospital
Speaker & Agent Coach || Delivering seminars and presentations to the public and Realtors about buying and selling real estate since 1995.

FREE CONDO SELLER REFERENCE MATERIAL

I've recently written a book for Toronto condominium owners and sellers to help them through the condo selling process.

Throughout this **Breakthrough Marketing With A Guaranteed Difference** package we will be often referring to actions you can take to improve your sale price and increase your understanding of the condo selling process.

This BREAKTHROUGH MARKETING package is meant as a guide and doesn't go into great detail on some of the topics covered. However, you can use my **Insider Tips To Getting The Best Price** book as your reference guide while you are reading.

Topics in this package that are relevant to chapters in the book itself will be highlighted at the bottom of the article with **HOMEWork** and a relevant page(s) reference from the book.

If you don't have the paper-back book handy, you can download the free PDF version at **GettingTheBestPrice.ca**.

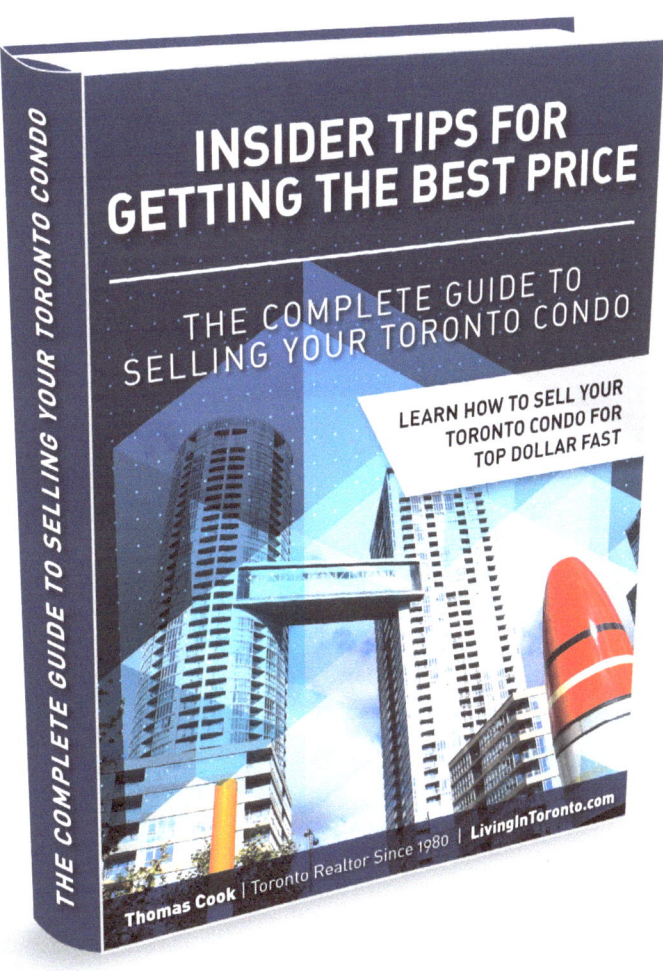

WE'RE APPLYING FOR THE IMPORTANT JOB
AS YOUR TRUSTED REALTOR

You need the best Realtor representation when your home goes on the market for sale.

Has it occurred to you that real estate agents seem to have become a 'commodity' in recent years? In some cases, it's absolutely true. Barriers to becoming a licensed agent are quite low.

With 48,000+ Realtors in the Toronto Real Estate Board now, an increase of 20,000 in the past several years, there are many who are inexperienced. Statistics show that 93% of all sales are done by just 7% of the agents.

You know the expression 'buying or selling a home is one of the largest transactions you'll make in your life'. Do you want to entrust that 'largest transaction' to be carried out by someone who may be unfamiliar with all the nuances of the sales and negotiation process?

Instead of employing someone randomly, you should give consideration to your listing agent's skill levels and how they're differentiated based on the following attributes.

Be sure that the agent you want to represent your best interests has…

- ✓ Honesty above all else - putting the interests of their client first
- ✓ The experience and proven results you want your agent to have
- ✓ Proficiency in pricing homes correctly for the market we're currently in
- ✓ Provided advice on how to make your home look the best it possibly can
- ✓ Counselled you with expert knowledge of the entire home buying process
- ✓ Creative marketing skills to draw the attention of the perfect buyer
- ✓ Skills in using cutting-edge technology for all facets of their business
- ✓ Systems in place to make every part of the selling process run smoothly
- ✓ Guarantees of service to give you confidence that few things will go wrong
- ✓ Regular agent-seller communications to keep the owner up-to-date on what's happening in the market
- ✓ Know-how to be an excellent mediator and strong negotiator to get the best price and offer terms for your home

As you'll see from this Breakthrough Marketing proposal, we've got ALL the skills you want and need to make your sale a financial success.

Please read over this marketing proposal and see if you agree that having Toronto's Real Estate Team (Thomas Cook and Partners) at RE/MAX represent you is the perfect fit to get your home sold successfully.

FIRST THINGS FIRST…

We've been in this business since 1980 and after listening to our clients over the years, we've learned a few things about what you want as a condo seller.

Here's What YOU, As Home Sellers, Have Told Us…

You want…

- **The best price possible for your home in the current market**
- **A quick sale within your time frame**
- **Limited hassles — and the entire process to be as stress-free as possible**
- **To trust that your Realtor is always working with YOUR best interests at heart**

Because this is what YOU want from a Realtor, this is what we strive to provide.

We hope that the information contained in this **Breakthrough Marketing Program** booklet outlines exactly how we work hard to meet YOUR goals.

You can read information about our current market, the "23 Great Questions To Ask A Realtor Before Signing Any Listing Agreement", the all-important PPPN principles for selling a property and a description of the way Toronto's Real Estate Team does business.

We've also included copies of our personal Guarantees of Service, details of how our Breakthrough Marketing Program works and a list of the information we need from you to get your property marketed and sold for the highest possible price.

So, read on, build your knowledge and, if you feel like I've added some value to you, please get the information together that we'll need (see page 31 in this proposal) to move forward and put your home on the market.

Your 'preferred' Toronto Realtor,

Thomas Cook

CONTENTS

1	List With The Best - RE/MAX Hallmark Dominates Toronto's Real Estate Market	1
2	What's Happening In Our Local Toronto Real Estate Market?	3
3	Home Seller Timeline Explained	4
4	A Formula For Success… The PPPN Principles Of Listing	6
5	Increase Your Home's Value With Simple Cosmetic Fix-Ups!	8
6	First Impressions Are Critical To Maximizing Your Home's Value!	9
7	Our 'By Referral Only' Business Philosophy	10
8	The Selling Process Needs To Move At YOUR Pace	11
9	If Everything Could Be Perfect… Describe Your Ultimate Home Selling Scenario	12
10	What's So Different About Our Real Estate Team	13
11	What Sets Toronto's Real Estate Team Apart…	14
12	Our Guarantees Of Service	18
13	We're Sticklers For Excellent Client Communication	21
14	It's Now Time To Put Your Home On The Market	22
15	Listing Agreement – Plain English	23
16	Happy Client List Here Are Some 'True Stories'	27
17	We Know That Cash In Your Pocket Is Important!	29
18	If You Decide To 'Hire' Toronto's Real Estate Team – Thomas Cook & Partners	30
19	Seller Homework - 'If you were the buyer…'	31
20	23 Great Questions To Ask A Realtor Before Signing Any Listing Agreement	33
21	We Progress Along With Technology…	37
22	Breakthrough Marketing Program	38
23	We Guarantee That You Will Sell Your Home For Thousands More	41
24	**Are You Also A Toronto Condo Or House Buyer?**	42
25	Chapter Titles From Our 'Insider Tips For Getting The Best Price' Book	43

LIST WITH THE BEST - RE/MAX HALLMARK DOMINATES TORONTO'S REAL ESTATE MARKET

RE/MAX Hallmark was founded in 1980 on three guiding principles:

Hallmark helps its agents by providing state of the art technology, leadership, and training in all aspects of the real estate industry. Their leadership team, staff and associates are dedicated to help agents succeed in their career.

RE/MAX Hallmark is extremely proud of our industry and take on the responsibility of helping to grow our industry in the heart and minds of our consumers. We expect and deliver professional service and care to everyone we are privileged to serve.

We make a difference in our communities. We are engaged - making a difference in every way we can. Our realtors and staff raise over $250,000 yearly in support of various initiatives - as close as your neighbourhood and as far away as needed.

Hallmark currently has over 1,200 agents in 9 offices in the Greater Toronto Area and 4 others in Ottawa.

I've been proud to be a long-time Realtor with the company since I joined in June of 1983 and I've watched and participated in the company's growth ever since.

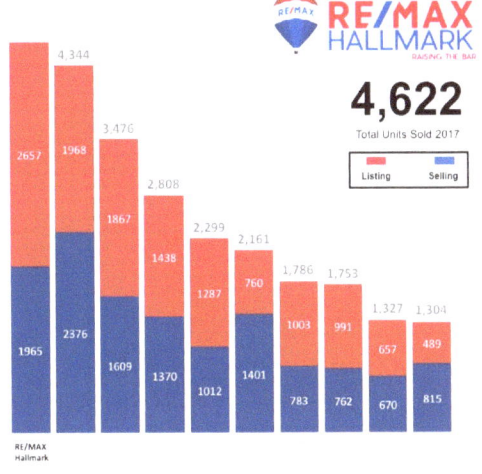
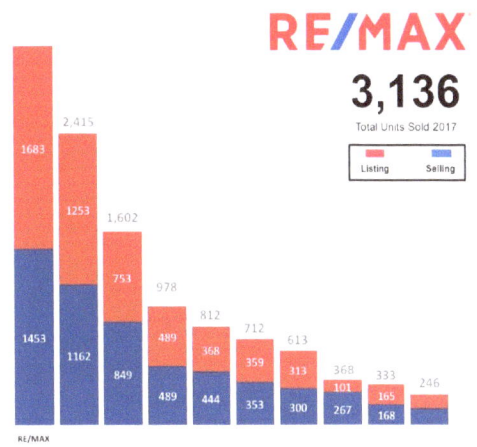

By listing with Toronto's Real Estate Team, you're also enlisting the support of all the company's GTA agents to get your home sold.

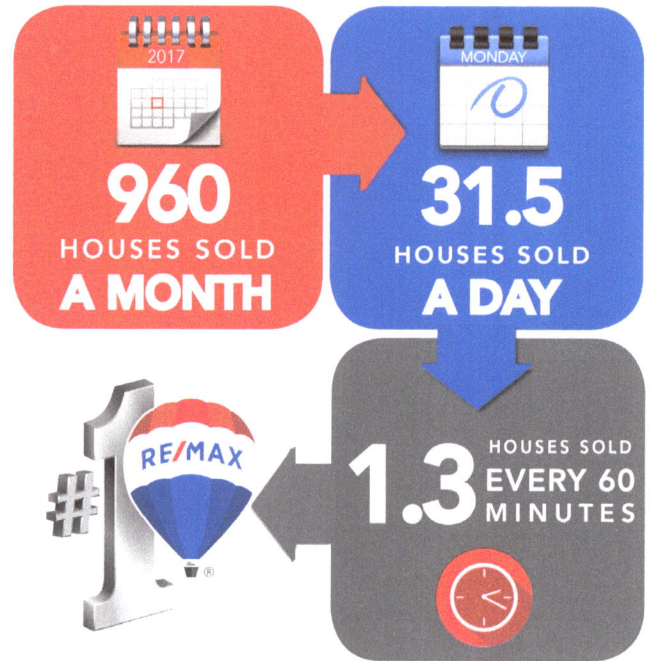

I've been working for Hallmark since June 1983 and I've had the privilege of getting to know many of the Realtors in the company and I've taught many classes for them.

Whenever a Hallmark agent gets a listing throughout the GTA, the other company Realtors are notified that same day and everyone cooperates to get that home sold quickly and for an excellent price.

WHAT'S HAPPENING IN OUR LOCAL TORONTO REAL ESTATE MARKET?

The newspapers and media are often commenting about what Toronto's market is doing but just sometimes they don't have it quite right.

You need to hear about what's happening from the 'horse's mouth' as it were.

Toronto's Real Estate Team is diligent in tracking the Toronto Real Estate Board statistics monthly. We even create infographics to help buyers and sellers keep up to date with what's happening.

Since the stats are constantly changing monthly, we can't keep them updated here. However, on our popular website **LivingInToronto.com**, we post blog articles monthly with a video report of what's happening including all the stats you'd ever want.

Go to our site to get an overview and we'll talk in person about what's happening in your particular neighbourhood. Check it out here… LivingInToronto.com/blog.

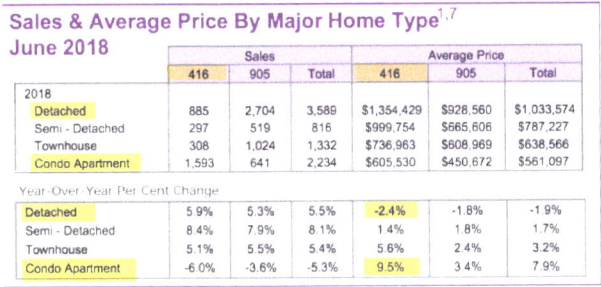

HOME SELLER TIMELINE EXPLAINED

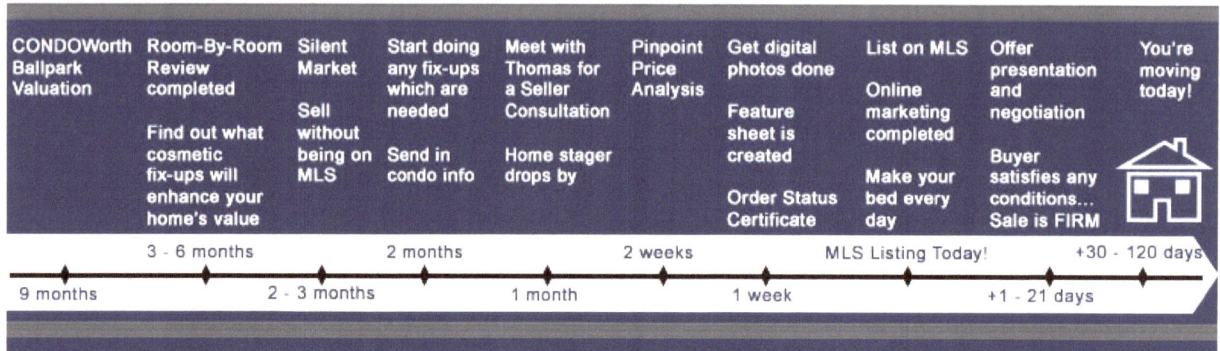

People approach selling their properties with multiple timelines… some make a snap decision and want it on the market the day after tomorrow while others know the time is coming and they give themselves a few weeks and sometimes even a month or two to get the home prepared for sale.

There is certainly no minimum built into the system. A home owner could sign the paperwork tonight and be on the MLS tomorrow morning - maybe not the best idea because the marketing might not be complete, or even started, but it could be done.

The selling process works best if you allow some lead time before the listing is loaded onto the Toronto Real Estate Board (TREB) MLS system.

Let's look at the timeline above which is a demonstration of how we like to progress with our seller clients at whatever pace works for them.

Many sellers start off with just a random thought of moving so they go online several months ahead of their listing date to start researching home values.

The next question that typically crosses their mind is **'What improvements or fix-ups should I do to maximize my sale price?'**.

Here's where some expert advice comes in handy because we've seen owners spend more money than they should have doing upgrades which the buying public may not like or which may not be necessary.

We've created what we call a **Room-By-Room Review** where we do a walk-through of your home with you. We'll suggest cosmetic-only fix-ups and answer your questions as to what other changes or improvements would bring you a better return on the money you spend.

Some sellers have been open to having a limited number of qualified buyers access their home before it officially goes on the market… we call it our 'Silent Market'. Since we have a large database of buyers, this less stressful and less intrusive way of getting a home sold appeals to some sellers.

Once the **Room-By-Room Review** has been done, the seller now knows very specifically what they need to do to get prepared for selling and they can typically attach a realistic timeline to it. It may be just a few days or it might be a few weeks or even months before the things on the fix-up / cleanup list can be completed. No problem… whatever works best.

When the time comes to put the home officially on the market, the next step is to have a Seller Consultation where we'll review the fix-ups that have been completed, talk about current market conditions, go over our marketing plan and look at comparable sales that have happened recently.

Then the listing documents are signed and we've got a specific date set for when the home is going to be listed for sale officially. Our marketing program is put in place and is ready for that listing date.

We'll look at offers as per our seller's instructions and of course, negotiate on their behalf.

The closing date is usually within 30-60 days of the offer acceptance date although shorter or longer closings are possible.

A FORMULA FOR SUCCESS…
THE PPPN PRINCIPLES OF LISTING

Every industry has its formulas for success and real estate is no exception. These formulas are, for the most part, not taught in any real estate school or seminar, although they are not a secret to the most successful Realtors in the business. If you asked them, most agents wouldn't even be able to tell you what the successful formula is for getting a client's listing sold for the best possible price.

The formula that we've created is **PPPN**, which stands for **Pricing, Presentation, Promotion and Negotiation**. All four components are decisive for getting your home sold in any type of market! It requires the owner and the agent to work together to discuss the proper pricing of the property (and set the list price 3-5% above market value to allow for negotiating room) and to show the owner how s/he can improve the presentation of their home cosmetically and inexpensively to increase its value and marketability.

Once these two key elements are in place, the promotion of the property takes place in several ways. First, we must get buyers excited about your home and interested in making an appointment to see it in person.

To maximize a buyer's online 'First Showing' experience, we market your property on Toronto's and the world's most popular real estate websites for listings in our city!

LivingInToronto.com
TorontoHomesAndCondos.com (our RE/MAX Hallmark office real estate site)
REMAX.ca
REMAX.com
Global.REMAX.com
and of course, Realtor.ca

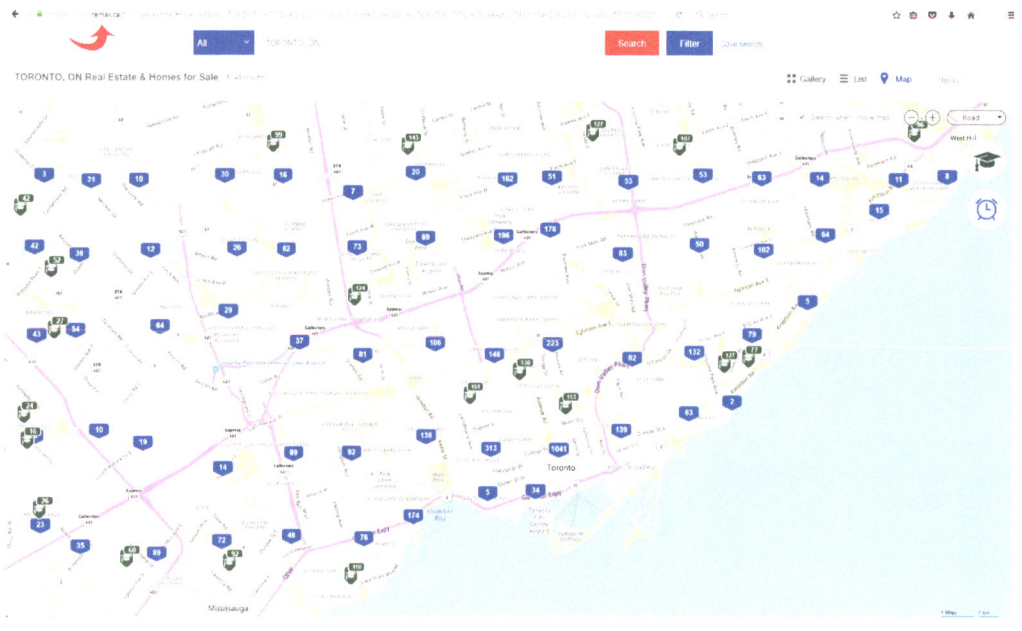

Once a buyer has made an appointment, we want to give them a 'WOW' when they walk in your door. One of the most important parts of the WOW (besides how you've presented your home) is providing a full-colour feature sheet for agents and buyers.

Our professional photographer takes digital pictures inside and out and we use them to create a 4-6 page colour feature sheet that includes a buyer cost-of-ownership spreadsheet, specific details about the qualities and features of your property (using your 'What I'll Miss the Most" list) PLUS lots of colour photos, as well as floor plans for your condo and a neighbourhood features page.

We will devote detailed webpages to your property on RE/MAX websites, as well as on our affiliated award-winning, high traffic website, **LivingInToronto.com** to attract Toronto buyers.

Hundreds of unique visitors a month will peruse up to 20 colour pictures of your home, along with a detailed description of your home's interior, an interactive Google map as well as a YouTube video and interactive virtual tour of your home... from the comfort of their living rooms.

Finally, once an offer is on the table, the actual negotiations between us and the buyer (through their agent) will definitively determine what price you get for your home.

When you have someone strong, knowledgeable and experienced in negotiations on "your team", you can't help but get a better price.

If any of these four PPPN steps are missed, or are executed poorly, you lose!

You must trust your agent's skill and experience in today's market to help you take full advantage and get the best possible price for your property. More than ever, experience is essential to getting you the highest value in a complex market!

Later in this Seller Breakthrough Marketing Program booklet you'll find a copy of our listing plan that outlines ALL that we do to ensure that your home gets sold for the best price — and as quickly as possible.

Before they recently put their home up for sale, Mike and Cathy spent a few weekends doing cosmetic touch-ups throughout their property. For instance, Mike repainted a portion of the kitchen ceiling where there had been a past leak (since repaired) and boxed up a bunch of 'extra' stuff — the kind that everyone accumulates over the years!

By the way… we always try to stick with just doing the cosmetics when recommending improvements that our sellers should make before selling.

We've found that it's the pretty homes that sell and that garner the highest price! Also, a sparkling clean and tidy home, as you can imagine, appeals to everyone.

INCREASE YOUR HOME'S VALUE WITH SIMPLE COSMETIC FIX-UPS!

NOW is a great time to get your home on the market. However, accurate pricing is important for all homes because every month a percentage of the houses and condos listed don't get sold.

Cosmetics are also critical... the interior of your condo should be as good as you can get it WITHOUT spending a lot of money.

Our Team listing specialists will be happy to do a Room-By-Room Review of your home to suggest quick and easy cosmetic-only repairs and touch-ups that will likely earn you $thousands in return.

Remember, you can spend a lot of money making the wrong renovations if you don't know what today's buyer wants in a condo residence.

The Buyer Specialist part of our Team helps several buyers every single month to find their "dream homes," so we know their desires firsthand.

Time after time we've found that those owners who follow our 'strictly cosmetic' fix-up tips to the letter get their home sold quicker and for absolute TOP dollar!

Our real estate marketing experience SINCE 1980 helps to get you the best price and you can take advantage of it without paying any more than what the typical agent charges!

FIRST IMPRESSIONS ARE CRITICAL TO MAXIMIZING YOUR HOME'S VALUE!

For starters, make sure your foyer is clean and bright.

Add vases of flowers everywhere. Dress up your dining room table with a couple of wine glasses and a bottle of champagne. If you have a balcony, put flowers out there too and prepare a nice seating area.

Steam clean the carpets and wash doors and walls as necessary.

Eliminate clutter and overcrowding in every room of your condo including closets.

This will assist in creating the impression of spaciousness throughout!

In a random survey, statistics revealed 82% of people who bought or sold a home had a miserable experience (Real Estate Marketing University) and they blamed it mainly on their real estate agent.

Preparing For A Showing

How To Prepare For A Showing In Ten Minutes Or Less

1. Put the dishes in the dishwasher (or quickly wash the dishes)
2. Make the beds
3. Wipe the counters
4. Empty the garbage
5. Hide dirty clothes in the washer or hamper
7. Take a deep breath
8. Run a quick vacuum
9. Turn on the lights
10. Open up all the window blinds / curtains
11. Leave your home before showings are set to start
12. Smile! You did it!

We're working hard to get your home sold and we appreciate your hard work too!!

OUR 'BY REFERRAL ONLY' BUSINESS PHILOSOPHY

At Toronto's Real Estate Team we have adopted a particular philosophy of doing business, which is called By Referral Only™. Our team members strive to provide such impeccable service and counsel that our clients will recommend us to friends, co-workers, family and acquaintances.

How do you benefit from this philosophy? It's simple… our business depends on giving you such top-notch, excellent service that you will happily sing our praises to anyone you know who is looking for a Realtor.

After all, most years between 50+ per cent of our business is referred to us by past clients. If we don't maintain our high standards and ensure that referrals keep coming our way, half of our business might disappear. The health of our business depends upon our quality of service!

Our clients also benefit from this philosophy because we devote more time to their needs and less time looking for new clients.

Most Realtors, unfortunately, do business as though they will never see or hear from their current clients again. That mindset can lead to shoddy service because the Realtor just wants to close a deal and move on to the next transaction.

Those Realtors don't build trust with clients and are afraid of losing them, which can lead them to push decisions on to their clients (which may not be in their client's best interest) in their haste to 'get the deal done.'

However, we at Toronto's Real Estate Team view our relationship with our clients as a long-term association. As Realtors, the more we know our clients, the better we can serve them. In some instances, we have counseled clients to **not sell their home**. Our Team members tell the truth — again and again — and live with the consequences. We have found that people prefer to work this way.

HOMEWork – Read Chapter 36 to learn more about this topic

THE SELLING PROCESS NEEDS TO MOVE AT YOUR PACE

Why are we willing to wait so patiently? Simple—we plan to be in the business for many more years! Whether you buy or sell now, in six months or in a few years from now makes no difference to us — we want you to proceed at a pace that you set.

If our clients can always count on us for unbiased, professional advice and they learn to trust and respect us, those clients are more likely to recommend us to other people. Once again, it comes around full circle to our By Referral Only business philosophy!

An additional bonus to Toronto's Real Estate Team's business philosophy is that they can readily recommend other 'By Referral Only' professionals whom home buyers and sellers might need to hire.

Over the years, we have built up a database of reliable, highly recommended people from renovators, to lawyers, to carpet cleaners, to insurance agents, in order to save our clients a lot of the leg work.

After all, who couldn't use the extra bit of time just when they are about to move homes, or to put their condominium on the market?

Our team members are firm believers in the By Referral Only business philosophy because it's a 'win-win' for everyone. We win by having a rewarding and successful business life and our clients win by getting impeccable service.

When you, as a property owner, start to think about selling your home or investment property, you really have just four options to consider...

See the chapter '**What's So Different About Our Real Estate Team**'.

IF EVERYTHING COULD BE PERFECT…
DESCRIBE YOUR ULTIMATE HOME SELLING SCENARIO

Do you have a clear vision or picture in your mind of what your home selling process looks like? Is it going to be an emotional journey for you or is it a less stressful jumping-off point to where you're going to be living next?

If you're trying to decide what's the best path for yourself going forward, go through the **'Ultimate Scenario'** questions below and you might just get some clarity…

What are the positives if you sell this property?

What are the negatives if you don't sell this property?

What is your biggest fear if you don't sell this property?

What is your biggest fear if you DO sell this property?

Imagine you've overcome these fears… describe how life would be different once your property is sold!

Is there any way that we can persuade you to keep this property?

In your opinion, what is the best way that Toronto's Real Estate Team can help you right now?

Are you willing to price your home so that it WILL sell, if that's your decision?

WHAT'S SO DIFFERENT ABOUT OUR REAL ESTATE TEAM?

One of the reasons people trust us more is that we offer you four options… not one.

And whichever one you choose is **OK** with us!

Option 1:

You may choose to do nothing right now. For whatever reason, you decide that the time is not right to sell your home in today's market

Option 2:

You could sell your property yourself – every year about 5% of the homes sold in Toronto are sold privately by their owners, usually to friends or family

Option 3:

You may decide to hire a "traditional" real estate salesperson to sell your home. There are now over 52,000 Realtors in the Toronto Real Estate Board – Membership has gone up over 20,000 since 2013 and the vast majority are inexperienced, doing only 1-5 sales per year

Option 4:

OR… You can choose to work with a group of professional, experienced real estate consultants and advisors, like Toronto's Real Estate Team, who do business on a 'By Referral Only' basis.

When you choose Option 4, you've made a wise decision to work with Realtors who are committed to not 'selling' you on anything!

Our team members will act as your real estate consultants and advisors… educating you, informing you, counseling you… to make sure you're a 'Smart, Educated Seller' and that you know all your options before you make a selling decision.

By working 'By Referral Only', our goal is to provide such excellent service and results that you will feel compelled to tell all your friends and family so they too can benefit from our expertise.

WHAT SETS TORONTO'S REAL ESTATE TEAM APART…

There are many factors that sets Toronto's Real Estate Team apart from most of the other 52,000 agents registered with the Toronto Real Estate Board. Here are just a few of them.

Copy Writing

Your home needs to be described and marketed in a professional way… both on the MLS listing itself and in the home's marketing materials. You do not want spelling or grammar mistakes to distract or impede getting a buyer interested in seeing your suite.

Copywriting is the art and science or writing copy (words used on web pages, ads, promotional materials, etc.) that sells your product or service and convinces prospective customers to take action. In many ways, it's like hiring one salesman to reach all your customers.

It's very important selling real estate, in your description of your listing, to have the right copywriting done correctly. This is where you engage and interact with the customer by certain words that are used and certain phrases that catch people's attention and **it sets you apart from just other listings**.

I've been writing descriptive and compelling real estate marketing for many years. Most recently since 2016, I've written three complete books about the Toronto home buying, mortgage financing and condo selling process.

Online Marketing In General

There has never been a time where your online marketing and presence means more than it does now. Conservatively, over **95% of buyers search for homes online**. That's how important it is to have a solid and consistent presence at every turn.

Marketing online to all generations means that websites must be mobile compatible and they must show up on multiple websites plus social media platforms too.

If an agent is not providing this benefit to potential clients, they're doing them a disservice.

Toronto's Real Estate Team has been a pioneer in having an online presence since 1998. We continue to do so to this day by providing easy access to the MLS and our Team listings and by offering a multitude of free reports, books and blog articles to help educate future home buyers and sellers.

Online Targeted Marketing

Targeted marketing lets us focus our search for buyers who have the right income, who have the correct jobs and who live, or want to live, in the Toronto neighbourhoods where we want our buyers to move to. When we're marketing to find buyers for your listing, we're not marketing to just everybody and we try to eliminate people who aren't qualified to purchase the home that you're listing.

Targeted marketing is the best solution for only drawing attention to serious buyers because we're hitting the nail on the head every time with these people. Online targeted marketing is tricky because it involves a detailed understanding of connecting with social circles, targeted behaviors, ad spend and blogging, partnering up and being relevant in your community.

It takes a little bit of time setting up our ads. It takes a little bit more time coming up with a list of who we want to target and make sure we're targeting the correct people who would be excited about seeing your home.

Listing Photography

Professional photography is probably the most important thing in presenting your listing to the public. Pictures of your home are the first thing that people look at when they're scrolling through the MLS, our website or our advertising on Facebook.

You want to make sure that your home is presented very well, that the lighting's done correctly and the photo angles are done correctly.

A good photograph has a significantly higher probability of getting a home sold when compared to a bad or even mediocre image. There's almost a **300% increase in clicks when the photographs are visually attractive**.

Toronto's Real Estate Team really wants to make sure that your home's photos look clean and stand out from the other MLS listings.

Presenting Your Home

If you stage your home well, it will stand out from your competition.

Should you stage your home? Definitely yes, but staging doesn't necessarily mean adding new furniture… more often it's decluttering, cleaning, doing cosmetic fix-ups and generally improving the look of the place.

The point is to make it look fresh and clean and feel like home. Just make it look as best as possible. This is a sure way to get buyers to submit offers quickly. The more offers there are means a better choice to get the most money at a much faster rate.

HOMEWork… Read over Chapters 2, 3, 4, 6, 7, 8, 9, 11 and 13 in our 'Insider Tips…' book to learn more about getting your home ready for the market

Videos And Virtual Tours

Photographs are great but they just cannot present what a video can present. A video presents your condominium as if the buyer were walking in the door themselves.

Some virtual tours are full videos while others show your home in a panoramic perspective from several positions in the suite. A third 'virtual' option is a stitching together of several still photos. If done professionally, this will often work too.

We will post your home's video / virtual tour to our website, the public Realtor.ca site and on our Facebook business page.

Floor Plan

If words alone don't help buyers visualize the home, and videos don't provide the details they want, then the floorplan is the ultimate game-changer.

Not only does it provide an elaborately detailed view of the home, but by adding color and illustrations of their potential furniture arrangements, **buyers are able to truly envision this home as the perfect place to settle in**.

Direct Mail

Direct mail still works if the message is creative and attention getting.

A well-designed postcard is great for mailing because they attract the reader's attention and are more personalized. They are especially useful for homes that just coming onto the market and they can help increase local awareness of properties on the market to those who are interested or know of someone who is.

Toronto's Real Estate Team has a database of condo investors who are continuing to add to their portfolio.
Property Feature Sheet

Breakthrough Marketing With A Guaranteed Difference

A full-colour 4- or 6-page feature sheet is a useful tool for the "let me think about it" buyer. These brochures have a long shelf life which can convince the interested prospect to buy your home instead of a competitor's.

Feature sheets are very important to hand out to potential buyers. We bring along a clear plastic stand to display the feature sheets and we ask our sellers to position that stand in a prominent location in their suite where it won't be missed.

We want the buyer to immediately pick it up when they enter and refer to it as they do their walk-through and after they've completed their showings for that day or evening.

Our feature sheets provide lots of colour photos, a written description of your condo suite and the amenities, plus a list of neighbourhood features to entice the buyer to consider your condo as their new home.

OUR GUARANTEES OF SERVICE

We offer two main guarantees that put the responsibility of providing good service back to the Realtor, which is where it belongs.

1. We'll allow you to cancel your listing at any time if you aren't satisfied with our level of service to you. (We've been told by some top agents that if they allowed their clients to do this, they would lose half of their listings.)

    We are committed to providing you with the best of everything with our Breakthrough Marketing Program that includes PPPN... our counseling you about Pricing and Presentation—and our Promotion and Negotiating skills that ultimately gets you the best price!

2. We will be in touch weekly to let you know what has been happening during the previous seven days... even if we didn't have any showings whatsoever.

    We will outline: what we did to market your property, the number of showings and buyers' responses to your home. For every call that we miss, we take $50 off our commission.

In addition, we listen to what you have to say. We want to know what your concerns are, what questions you have and how we can best help you!

We're concerned that you be educated and informed about the market... that you be confident that you're making the right decision for YOUR personal circumstances.

Once you realize that we won't pressure you into doing anything that you don't want to do, there's a major turning point in our relationship... trust has been established between us!

YOU will be more open with us... more revealing about what really concerns you and that, in turn, allows us to better counsel you and give you the excellent advice that you need and deserve.

You Can Fire Us Anytime!
No Hassle, Easy Exit Listing Cancellation Guarantee

Occasionally, Sellers list their homes with agents and regret their decision later ... sometimes they realize that their Realtor is less than competent or has mislead them about market values, or that their Realtor has not updated them regularly with feedback about their home.

Here's What You Can Expect From Our Team...

We guarantee that you can **FIRE US** and cancel your Listing Contract **ANYTIME** if you're not satisfied with our service.

No Hassles, No Conditions - It's Easy

We take away the risk and fear by guaranteeing, **IN WRITING**, that you can fire us and end your listing with us at any time if you are not satisfied with our service.

We're Confident You Won't Need It...

You can enjoy the calibre of service that you deserve, from Realtors who are confident enough to make this type of guarantee...

Realtors who work 'By Referral Only'

Seller's Name (s)	
Property Address	
Signature	

Thomas Cook
Sales Rep at RE/MAX Hallmark Realty Ltd Brokerage
647-962-1650 Thomas@LivingInToronto.com

100% On Time
Showings & Marketing Feedback Guarantee

Toronto's Real Estate Team @ RE/MAX realize that one of the most common complaints made by sellers when listing their homes and using the services of a Realtor is that they rarely hear from their agent after the listing has been signed... sometimes not until the listing has almost expired, or an offer is made for their home.

The problem is that sellers often have NO idea what people are thinking about their home and they are left completely in the dark!

We Guarantee That We'll Be In Touch Continuously !
If we don't report back to you at a minimum of once every week (Monday thru Friday) until your property is sold, with either a telephone call or email outlining the previous week's showing and marketing activity for your property....

We promise to deduct $50 from our sales commission for every time that we're late with feedback, payable on closing day!

Seller(s) Names:

Property Address:

Signature:

Thomas Cook
**Sales Representative at
RE/MAX Hallmark Realty Ltd Brokerage**

647-962-1650
Thomas@LivingInToronto.com

WE'RE STICKLERS FOR EXCELLENT CLIENT COMMUNICATION

Many agents have a problem with communicating to their client what to expect during the sale of their condominium. We believe that the more you know about the process, the less stress you'll have and the better sleep you'll get at night while your suite is on the market.

To keep us organized and our service level to you very high, we've created several checklists to follow covering many facets of the home selling process.

We've got a checklist for dealing with tenanted suites as well as ones for owner-occupied condos.

Here's our '**After The Listing Is Signed**' checklist which we'll review with you to ensure that all the 'i's are dotted and the t's are crossed' when it comes to understanding what to expect.

Things To Cover With The Seller

- Set a time/date for the FLOOR PLANS to be done
- Set a time/date for iGuide to come over for photos / virtual tour
- Review the Listing Info Req'd sheets - all improvements noted?
- Get list of the building amenities
- Get key from seller and install lockbox (special key location @ condo bldg?)
- Get the "What I'll Miss The Most" form from the sellers
- Get all CONDO expense costs - EXACT realty taxes, utilities, maintenance fees
- Verify what's included in the maintenance fees
- Best closing date?
- Bridge financing discussion?
- ORDER STATUS CERTIFICATE - talk about importance of ordering Status & timing - what to do when it's ready for pickup
- PARKING & LOCKER - what are the parking space and locker numbers
- Discuss typical showing times Mon-Fri and on weekends
- Discuss how buyer appointments are set @ the RMX office
- Buyer showings - what to do/say & NOT say when buyer comes
- Team 17-21 day 'on the market' test period
- When do photos & video appear on TREB and on Realtor.ca ?
- OFFER process – what to expect! Email/printer/fax available at home?
- Keeping Feature Sheet stand filled – call for a re-supply a few days ahead

IT'S NOW TIME TO PUT YOUR HOME ON THE MARKET

OK, you've made the right decision to list your property with Toronto's Real Estate Team. Now it's time for all the paperwork to be signed.

The primary one is the MLS Listing Agreement which authorizes the agent to list your home on the Toronto Real Estate Board.

There's a copy of the 'plain English' version on the following pages for you to read but there are some common questions that you should have the answers to.

First is the length of the listing period. The minimum is 60 days although, in slow markets, some agents take a listing for much longer – it could be 6 months or more.

Most often for our Team, we just take the minimum period because the property will either sell OR it will need a price adjustment to get it sold.

In that case we always recommend that we cancel the old listing and relist fresh at the new price. That way the 'days-on-market' counter will again start at 'zero'.

The commission in clause 2 is of course negotiable depending on the level of service that you want. We typically recommend that the commission to the buyer agent be 2.5% to ensure that they show your home to their best clients.

See pages 38 to 40 for a description of our various Breakthrough Marketing service options and the percentage considerations that apply to each.

The seller will also be asked to sign several other documents as well including…

1- Individual Identification Information Record or FINTRAC form – part of the government's anti-money-laundering efforts – you'll need to provide identity proof such as a driver's license or passport

2- Working With A Realtor form – this makes it clear who is working for whom in the transaction. Most sellers want their agent to be working fully on their behalf during the sale but there are other options available

Please read over the plain English listing agreement in detail and make a note of any points that you might want clarification on.

REVIEW THE LISTING AGREEMENT – IN PLAIN ENGLISH

 **Listing Agreement**
Form 200
for use in the Province of Ontario
Seller Representation Agreement
Authority to Offer for Sale

GENERAL USE: This Form is a contract between a Seller and a real estate company that gives the real estate company permission to act on the Seller's behalf when they offer their home for sale in the open market. A written agreement is necessary in order to secure commission and to ensure compliance with the REBBA Code of Ethics.

This section of the Agreement identifies the parties involved and specifies the time period for the contract. If the time period is greater than six months then the Real Estate and Business Brokers Act and the Real Estate Council of Ontario require that the Seller(s) initial in the oval beside the bracket. There is also a statement in the form of a representation or warranty stating that the Sellers are party to another contract whether a Listing or an agreement to pay commission.

This is a Multiple Listing Service® Agreement (Seller's Initials) **OR** **Exclusive Listing Agreement** **EXCLUSIVE** (Seller's Initials)

BETWEEN:
BROKERAGE: ....
....(the "Listing Brokerage") Tel.No. (............)..

SELLER(S): ....(the "Seller")

In consideration of the Listing Brokerage listing the real property **for sale** known as..................................
....(the "Property")

the Seller hereby gives the Listing Brokerage the **exclusive and irrevocable** right to act as the Seller's agent, **commencing** at 12:01 a.m. on the .... day of ...., 20........, **until** 11:59 p.m. on the .... day of ...., 20........ (the "Listing Period"),

{ Seller acknowledges that the length of the Listing Period is negotiable between the Seller and the Listing Brokerage and, if an MLS® listing, may be subject to minimum requirements of the real estate board, however, in accordance with the Real Estate and Business Brokers Act (2002), **if the Listing Period exceeds six months, the Listing Brokerage must obtain the Seller's initials.** } (Seller's Initials)

to offer the Property **for sale** at a price of: .... Dollars (CDN$) ....

....Dollars

and upon the terms particularly set out herein, or at such other price and/or terms acceptable to the Seller. It is understood that the price and/or terms set out herein are at the Seller's personal request, after full discussion with the Listing Brokerage's representative regarding potential market value of the Property.

The Seller hereby represents and warrants that the Seller is not a party to any other listing agreement for the Property or agreement to pay commission to any other real estate brokerage for the sale of the Property.

1. DEFINITIONS AND INTERPRETATIONS: This paragraph clarifies the terms used in the Agreement and defines Buyer and Seller as they are referred to in the document.

1. **DEFINITIONS AND INTERPRETATIONS:** For the purposes of this Agreement ("Authority" or "Agreement"):
"Seller" includes vendor, a "buyer" includes a purchaser, and a prospective purchaser. A "real estate board" includes a real estate association. A purchase shall be deemed to include the entering into of any agreement to exchange, or the obtaining of an option to purchase which is subsequently exercised. Commission shall be deemed to include other remuneration. This Agreement shall be read with all changes of gender or number required by the context. For purposes of this Agreement, anyone introduced to or shown the Property shall be deemed to include any spouse, heirs, executors, administrators, successors, assigns, related corporations and affiliated corporations. Related corporations or affiliated corporations shall include any corporation where one half or a majority of the shareholders, directors or officers of the related or affiliated corporation are the same person(s) as the shareholders, directors, or officers of the corporation introduced to or shown the Property.

2. COMMISSION: An important section of the Agreement as it sets out fee that will be paid to real estate company. It also authorizes the real estate company to cooperate with any other real estate companies in order to sell the property. This section details how the commission paid to the Listing real estate company will be shared with the cooperating real estate company. In addition there is a period after the expiry of the Agreement where the real estate company would be entitled to commission if the Buyer was introduced to or shown the property during the contract period. This is the "holdover period".

2. **COMMISSION:** In consideration of the Listing Brokerage listing the Property, the Seller agrees to pay the Listing Brokerage a commission of ....% of the sale price of the Property or .... for any valid offer to purchase the Property from any source whatsoever obtained during the Listing Period and on the terms and conditions set out in this Agreement **OR** such other terms and conditions as the Seller may accept. The Seller authorizes the Listing Brokerage to co-operate with any other registered real estate brokerage (co-operating brokerage) to offer to pay the co-operating brokerage a commission of................% of the sale price

INITIALS OF LISTING BROKERAGE: **INITIALS OF SELLER(S):**

of the Property or……………………………………………………………………………….. out of the commission the Seller pays the Listing Brokerage.

The Seller further agrees to pay such commission as calculated above if an agreement to purchase is agreed to or accepted by the Seller or anyone on the Seller's behalf within …………………….. days after the expiration of the Listing Period (**Holdover Period**), so long as such agreement is with anyone who was introduced to the Property from any source whatsoever during the Listing Period or shown the Property during the Listing Period. If, however, the offer for the purchase of the Property is pursuant to a new agreement in writing to pay commission to another registered real estate brokerage, the Seller's liability for commission shall be reduced by the amount paid by the Seller under the new agreement.

The Seller further agrees to pay such commission as calculated above even if the transaction contemplated by an agreement to purchase agreed to or accepted by the Seller or anyone on the Seller's behalf is not completed, if such non-completion is owing to or attributable to the Seller's default or neglect, said commission to be payable on the date set for completion of the purchase of the Property.

Any deposit in respect of any agreement where the transaction has been completed shall first be applied to reduce the commission payable. Should such amounts paid to the Listing Brokerage from the deposit or by the Seller's solicitor not be sufficient, the Seller shall be liable to pay to the Listing Brokerage on demand, any deficiency in commission and taxes owing on such commission.

All amounts set out as commission are to be paid plus applicable taxes on such commission.

3. *REPRESENTATION: This paragraph confirms that the real estate company and the salesperson have explained the different types of agency relationships that may occur in a real estate transaction.*

3. **REPRESENTATION:** The Seller acknowledges that the Listing Brokerage has provided the Seller with information explaining agency relationships, including information on Seller Representation, Sub-agency, Buyer Representation, Multiple Representation and Customer Service.

The Seller understands that unless the Seller is otherwise informed, the co-operating brokerage is representing the interests of the buyer in the transaction. The Seller further acknowledges that the Listing Brokerage may be listing other properties that may be similar to the Seller's Property and the Seller hereby consents to the Listing Brokerage listing other properties that may be similar to the Seller's Property without any claim by the Seller of conflict of interest. The Seller hereby appoints the Listing Brokerage as the Seller's agent for the purpose of giving and receiving notices pursuant to any offer or agreement to purchase the Property. Unless otherwise agreed in writing between Seller and Listing Brokerage, any commission payable to any other brokerage shall be paid out of the commission the Seller pays the Listing Brokerage, said commission to be disbursed in accordance with the Commission Trust Agreement.

MULTIPLE REPRESENTATION: The Seller hereby acknowledges that the Listing Brokerage may be entering into buyer representation agreements with buyers who may be interested in purchasing the Seller's Property. In the event that the Listing Brokerage has entered into or enters into a buyer representation agreement with a prospective buyer for the Seller's Property, the Listing Brokerage will obtain the Seller's written consent to represent both the Seller and the buyer for the transaction at the earliest practicable opportunity and in all cases prior to any offer to purchase being submitted or presented.

The Seller understands and acknowledges that the Listing Brokerage must be impartial when representing both the Seller and the buyer and equally protect the interests of the Seller and buyer. The Seller understands and acknowledges that when representing both the Seller and the buyer, the Listing Brokerage shall have a duty of full disclosure to both the Seller and the buyer, including a requirement to disclose all factual information about the Property known to the Listing Brokerage.

However, the Seller further understands and acknowledges that the Listing Brokerage shall not disclose:
- that the Seller may or will accept less than the listed price, unless otherwise instructed in writing by the Seller;
- that the buyer may or will pay more than the offered price, unless otherwise instructed in writing by the buyer;
- the motivation of or personal information about the Seller or buyer, unless otherwise instructed in writing by the party to which the information applies or unless failure to disclose would constitute fraudulent, unlawful or unethical practice;
- the price the buyer should offer or the price the Seller should accept; and
- the Listing Brokerage shall not disclose to the buyer the terms of any other offer.

However, it is understood that factual market information about comparable properties and information known to the Listing Brokerage concerning potential uses for the Property will be disclosed to both Seller and buyer to assist them to come to their own conclusions.

Where a Brokerage represents both the Seller and the Buyer (multiple representation), the Brokerage shall not be entitled or authorized to be agent for either the Buyer or the Seller for the purpose of giving and receiving notices.

MULTIPLE REPRESENTATION AND CUSTOMER SERVICE: The Seller understands and agrees that the Listing Brokerage also provides representation and customer service to other sellers and buyers. If the Listing Brokerage represents or provides customer service to more than one seller or buyer for the same trade, the Listing Brokerage shall, in writing, at the earliest practicable opportunity and before any offer is made, inform all sellers and buyers of the nature of the Listing Brokerage's relationship to each seller and buyer.

4. *FINDERS FEES: In order for a Salesperson to receive any finder's fee it is necessary to receive consent. This section provides that consent. This may occur where a mortgage company sends a referral fee.*

4. **FINDERS FEES:** The Seller acknowledges that the Brokerage may be receiving a finder's fee, reward and/or referral incentive, and the Seller consents to any such benefit being received and retained by the Brokerage in addition to the Commission as described above.

5. *REFERRAL OF ENQUIRIES: This section requires that the Seller is to advise the real estate company of any enquiries made with respect to the property. If the enquiry results in an accepted offer to purchase during the listing period or after, during the holdover period, the Seller will be liable to pay commission.*

5. **REFERRAL OF ENQUIRIES:** The Seller agrees that during the Listing Period, the Seller shall advise the Listing Brokerage immediately of all enquiries from any source whatsoever, and all offers to purchase submitted to the Seller shall be immediately submitted to the Listing Brokerage before the Seller accepts or rejects the same. If any enquiry during the Listing Period results in the Seller accepting a valid offer to purchase during the Listing Period or within the Holdover Period after the expiration of the Listing Period, the Seller agrees to pay the Listing Brokerage the amount of Commission set out above, payable within five (5) days following the Listing Brokerage's written demand therefor.

INITIALS OF LISTING BROKERAGE: ⬭   **INITIALS OF SELLER(S):** ⬭

6. *MARKETING: The real estate brokerage is authorized to market the property. To do this there is permission to place a "For Sale" and "Sold" sign on the property.*
6. **MARKETING:** The Seller agrees to allow the Listing Brokerage to show and permit prospective buyers to fully inspect the Property during reasonable hours and the Seller gives the Listing Brokerage the sole and exclusive right to place "For Sale" and "Sold" sign(s) upon the Property. The Seller consents to the Listing Brokerage including information in advertising that may identify the Property. The Seller further agrees that the Listing Brokerage shall have sole and exclusive authority to make all advertising decisions relating to the marketing of the Property for sale during the Listing Period. The Seller agrees that the Listing Brokerage will not be held liable in any manner whatsoever for any acts or omissions with respect to advertising by the Listing Brokerage or any other party, other than by the Listing Brokerage's gross negligence or wilful act.

7. *WARRANTY: This warranty confirms that the Seller has all the authority necessary in order to sign the Listing. It also confirms that the Seller has disclosed outside interests such as first rights of refusal, easements, mortgages and so forth.*
7. **WARRANTY:** The Seller represents and warrants that the Seller has the exclusive authority and power to execute this Authority to offer the Property for sale and that the Seller has informed the Listing Brokerage of any third party interests or claims on the Property such as rights of first refusal, options, easements, mortgages, encumbrances or otherwise concerning the Property, which may affect the sale of the Property.

8. *INDEMNIFICATION AND INSURANCE: The Seller will not hold the Listing Brokerage liable for loss or damage to the property or contents unless it was caused by the Listing Brokerage's gross negligence or a willful act. Further the Seller confirms that the Seller has insurance to cover any injury or property damage that may occur.*
8. **INDEMNIFICATION AND INSURANCE:** The Seller will not hold the Listing Brokerage and representatives of the Brokerage responsible for any loss or damage to the Property or contents occurring during the term of this Agreement caused by the Listing Brokerage or anyone else by any means, including theft, fire or vandalism, other than by the Listing Brokerage's gross negligence or wilful act. The Seller agrees to indemnify and save harmless the Listing Brokerage and representatives of the Brokerage and any co-operating brokerage from any liability, claim, loss, cost, damage or injury, including but not limited to loss of the Commission payable under this Agreement, caused or contributed to by the breach of any warranty or representation made by the Seller in this Agreement or the accompanying data form. The Seller warrants the Property is insured, including personal liability insurance against any claims or lawsuits resulting from bodily injury or property damage to others caused in any way on or at the Property and the Seller indemnifies the Brokerage and all of its employees, representatives, salespersons and brokers (Listing Brokerage) and any co-operating brokerage and all of its employees, representatives, salespersons and brokers (co-operating brokerage) for and against any claims against the Listing Brokerage or co-operating brokerage made by anyone who attends or visits the Property.

9. *THE FAMILY LAW ACT: The Seller is warranting that if spousal consent is necessary then the spouse has signed this agreement.*
9. **FAMILY LAW ACT:** The Seller hereby warrants that spousal consent is not necessary under the provisions of the Family Law Act, R.S.O. 1990, unless the spouse of the Seller has executed the consent hereinafter provided.

10. *VERIFICATION OF INFORMATION: This section authorizes the Salesperson to obtain information from governments, mortgagees and others in order to help with the sale of the property.*
10. **VERIFICATION OF INFORMATION:** The Seller authorizes the Listing Brokerage to obtain any information affecting the Property from any regulatory authorities, governments, mortgagees or others and the Seller agrees to execute and deliver such further authorizations in this regard as may be reasonably required. The Seller hereby appoints the Listing Brokerage or the Listing Brokerage's authorized representative as the Seller's attorney to execute such documentation as may be necessary to effect obtaining any information as aforesaid. The Seller hereby authorizes, instructs and directs the above noted regulatory authorities, governments, mortgagees or others to release any and all information to the Listing Brokerage.

11. *USE AND DISTRIBUTION OF INFORMATION: This provision is necessary in order to facilitate the sale of the property. In order to ensure compliance with privacy laws the Seller consents to use and disclosure of personal information in order to market the property. This will include the use of photographs, surveys and so on.*
11. **USE AND DISTRIBUTION OF INFORMATION:** The Seller consents to the collection, use and disclosure of personal information by the Brokerage for the purpose of listing and marketing the Property including, but not limited to: listing and advertising the Property using any medium including the Internet; disclosing Property information to prospective buyers, brokerages, salespersons and others who may assist in the sale of the Property; such other use of the Seller's personal information as is consistent with listing and marketing of the Property. The Seller consents, if this is an MLS® Listing, to placement of the listing information and sales information by the Brokerage into the database(s) of the MLS® System of the appropriate Board, and to the posting of any documents and other information (including, without limitation, photographs, images, graphics, audio and video recordings, virtual tours, drawings, floor plans, architectural designs, artistic renderings, surveys and listing descriptions) provided by or on behalf of the Seller into the database(s) of the MLS® System of the appropriate Board. The Seller hereby indemnifies and saves harmless the Brokerage and/or any of its employees, servants, brokers or sales representatives from any and all claims, liabilities, suits, actions, losses, costs and legal fees caused by, or arising out of, or resulting from the posting of any documents or other information (including, without limitation, photographs, images, graphics, audio and video recordings, virtual tours, drawings, floor plans, architectural designs, artistic renderings, surveys and listing descriptions) as aforesaid. The Seller acknowledges that the database, within the board's MLS® System is the property of the real estate board(s) and can be licensed, resold, or otherwise dealt with by the board(s). The Seller further acknowledges that the real estate board(s) may: during the term of the listing and thereafter, distribute the information in the database, within the board's MLS® System to any persons authorized to use such service which may include other brokerages, government departments, appraisers, municipal organizations and others; market the Property, at its option, in any medium, including electronic media; during the term of the listing and thereafter, compile, retain and publish any statistics including historical data within the board's MLS® System and retain, reproduce and display photographs, images, graphics, audio and video recordings, virtual tours, drawings, floor plans, architectural designs, artistic renderings, surveys and listing descriptions which may be used by board members to conduct comparative analyses; and make such other use of the information as the Brokerage and/or real estate board(s) deem appropriate, in connection with the listing, marketing and selling of real estate during the term of the listing and thereafter. The Seller acknowledges that the information, personal or otherwise ("information"), provided to the real estate board or association may be stored on databases located outside of Canada, in which case the information would be subject to the laws of the jurisdiction in which the information is located.

INITIALS OF LISTING BROKERAGE: **INITIALS OF SELLER(S):**

Once a Listing has expired the Seller can choose to be contacted or not to be contacted by other real estate salespersons.

In the event that this Agreement expires or is cancelled or otherwise terminated and the Property is not sold, the Seller, by initialing:

consent to allow other real estate board members to contact the Seller after expiration or other termination of this Agreement to discuss listing or otherwise marketing the Property.

Does **Does Not**

12. SUCCESSORS AND ASSIGNS: This states that heirs, estate trustees or any other party legally acting on behalf of the Seller must also abide by the terms of this Agreement.
12. SUCCESSORS AND ASSIGNS: The heirs, executors, administrators, successors and assigns of the undersigned are bound by the terms of this Agreement.

13. CONFLICT OR DISCREPANCY: In the event something is added to the agreement, for example by way of schedule and the added part is in conflict or there is a discrepancy with a pre-printed clause, then the added part overrides the pre-printed provision.
13. CONFLICT OR DISCREPANCY: If there is any conflict or discrepancy between any provision added to this Agreement (including any Schedule attached hereto) and any provision in the standard pre-set portion hereof, the added provision shall supersede the standard pre-set provision to the extent of such conflict or discrepancy. This Agreement, including any Schedule attached hereto, shall constitute the entire Agreement between the Seller and the Listing Brokerage. There is no representation, warranty, collateral agreement or condition which affects this Agreement other than as expressed herein.

14. ELECTRONIC COMMUNICATION: This confirms that communications may occur electronically and will still be binding.
14. ELECTRONIC COMMUNICATION: This Agreement and any agreements, notices or other communications contemplated thereby may be transmitted by means of electronic systems, in which case signatures shall be deemed to be original. The transmission of this Agreement by the Seller by electronic means shall be deemed to confirm the Seller has retained a true copy of the Agreement.

15. ELECTRONIC SIGNATURES: This clause provides consent if the parties use electronic signatures with respect to this Agreement.
15. ELECTRONIC SIGNATURES: If this Agreement has been signed with an electronic signature the parties hereto consent and agree to the use of such electronic signature with respect to this Agreement pursuant to the *Electronic Commerce Act 2000, S.O. 2000, c17* as amended from time to time.

16. SCHEDULE(S): If something has been added such as a form, it should be noted here.
16. SCHEDULE(S): .... and data form attached hereto form(s) part of this Agreement.

This section provides that the listing company will market the property in order to obtain an offer acceptable to the Seller. The salesperson will sign the Listing on behalf of the brokerage.

THE LISTING BROKERAGE AGREES TO MARKET THE PROPERTY ON BEHALF OF THE SELLER AND REPRESENT THE SELLER IN AN ENDEAVOUR TO OBTAIN A VALID OFFER TO PURCHASE THE PROPERTY ON THE TERMS SET OUT IN THIS AGREEMENT OR ON SUCH OTHER TERMS SATISFACTORY TO THE SELLER.

.... DATE.................................... ....
(Authorized to bind the Listing Brokerage) (Name of Person Signing)

THIS AGREEMENT HAS BEEN READ AND FULLY UNDERSTOOD BY ME AND I ACKNOWLEDGE THIS DATE I HAVE SIGNED UNDER SEAL. Any representations contained herein or as shown on the accompanying data form respecting the Property are true to the best of my knowledge, information and belief.

SIGNED, SEALED AND DELIVERED I have hereunto set my hand and seal:

.... ● DATE ....
(Signature of Seller) (Seal) (Tel. No.)
.... ● DATE ....
(Signature of Seller) (Seal)

SPOUSAL CONSENT: The undersigned spouse of the Seller hereby consents to the listing of the Property herein pursuant to the provisions of the Family Law Act, R.S.O. 1990 and hereby agrees to execute all necessary or incidental documents to further any transaction provided for herein.

.... ● DATE ....
(Spouse) (Seal)

DECLARATION OF INSURANCE

The broker/salesperson...
(Name of Broker/Salesperson)
hereby declares that he/she is insured as required by the Real Estate and Business Brokers Act (REBBA) and Regulations.

....
(Signature(s) of Broker/Salesperson)

ACKNOWLEDGEMENT

The Seller(s) hereby acknowledge that the Seller(s) fully understand the terms of this Agreement and have received a true copy of this Agreement on the .... day of ...., 20 ....

.... Date: ....
(Signature of Seller)
.... Date: ....
(Signature of Seller)

The trademarks REALTOR®, REALTORS® and the REALTOR® logo are controlled by The Canadian Real Estate Association (CREA) and identify real estate professionals who are members of CREA. Used under license.

© 2017, Ontario Real Estate Association ("OREA"). All rights reserved. This form was developed by OREA for the use and reproduction by its members and licensees only. Any other use or reproduction is prohibited except with prior written consent of OREA. Do not alter when printing or reproducing the standard pre-set portion. OREA bears no liability for your use of this form.

Form 200   Revised 2017

HAPPY CLIENT LIST
HERE ARE SOME 'TRUE STORIES'

A 'Trust Specialist' Moves Back To Canada!

A few years ago, a Canadian couple living in North Carolina went online, found our website and signed up for our HOMEWatch Program.

As we got to know each other while we helped them to buy their lovely home, we learned that Darryl is one of North America's few specialists in the field of trust and negotiation and that his PhD thesis centred around the issue.

He was originally recruited by Duke University to be a professor and he moved back to Canada to accept a position with an investment company as their "building trust" and negotiating specialist!

Of course, we were thrilled that he and his wife Jill chose us to help them to buy a home, especially given Darryl's career specialty.

Darryl told us that the typical buyer of **anything** -- houses and condos included -- consciously or subconsciously asks themselves two questions…

1. How can I get 'screwed' in this transaction? (pardon the English), &

2. If I do get 'screwed', how bad will it be?

So, the natural next question that we asked him was "How did our Team answer those questions well enough so that you trusted us?"

There were several factors:

1. Our Guarantees of Service, specifically our 'You Can Fire Us Anytime' Buyer's Contract Easy Exit Guarantee and our Any Realtor Who Offers To Sell Your Home For Free Should Be Committed! guarantee. Having those guarantees in place (signed by us) let Darryl and Jill know that if anything were to go wrong with either their relationship with their Realtor (i.e. us), or with the home they bought, there were specific solutions to those concerns

2. The True Buyer Stories on our website and

3. They read the testimonial letters that past buyers and sellers have sent to us during the years

This gave Darryl and Jill concrete evidence of our history of providing a high level of customer service… they concluded that there was little 'risk' involved when hiring us.

It was a very satisfying experience for us because we earned the trust and respect of someone who studies trust and negotiating for a living. But most of all it was satisfying because we found Jill and Darryl a home that they were excited to buy and that they enjoy living in!

PS—Jill & Darryl ultimately sold their home with us and moved to BC :).

Even though this true story is from one of our buyers, the comments he makes about building trust and the importance of guarantees are just as important for a seller...

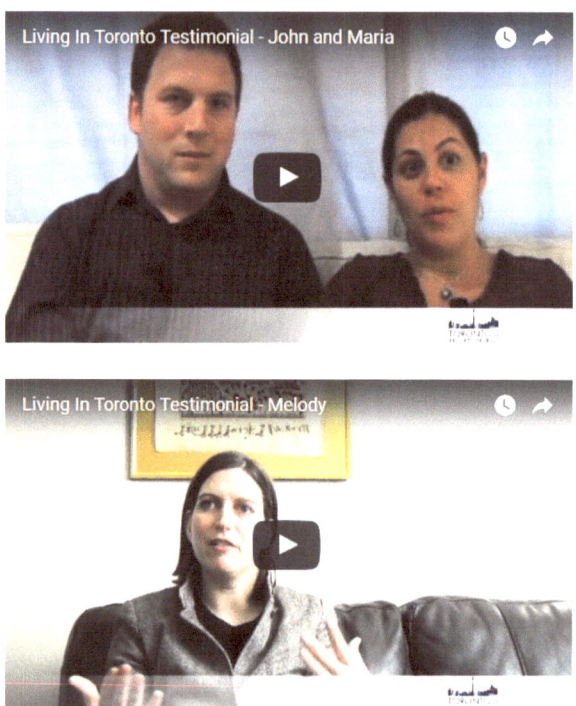

There are more videos from some of our clients available to watch on YouTube at
WhatPeopleAreSayingAboutUs.com.

WE KNOW THAT CASH IN YOUR POCKET IS IMPORTANT!

We realize that every person who sells their home is concerned about their 'bottom line" ... the amount that you will net after sales and closing costs.

What most sellers don't realize is that 90% of the time, the commission from the sale of your home is split 50/50 between two Realtors, the agent representing the Buyer and YOUR representative and advocate, the listing agent.

To incentivize the Buyer's Agent to show your home before others, he or she needs to receive ideally a minimum of 2.5% from the sale of your home!

Or... they just won't be bothered showing your home!

The balance of whatever commission is agreed upon is paid to your Listing Agent for the important work that he OR she does negotiating strongly on your behalf and all the expenses incurred in marketing your home.

Our Team's Professional Fee

It's not a secret. As you can see, our most common 5% professional fee is split between several different parties.

This is so we can offer you the best, most comprehensive services possible in order to get your condo sold in the least amount of time for the most amount of money.

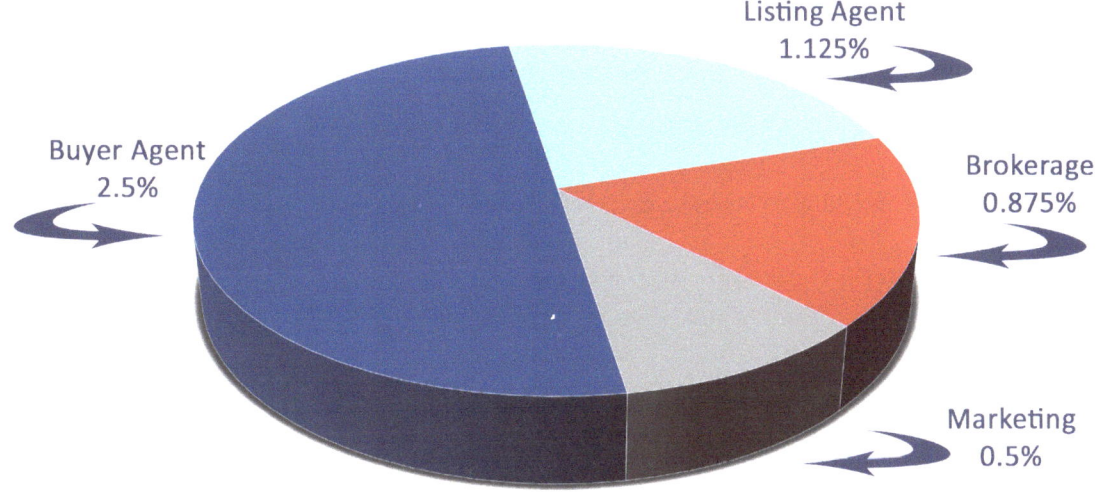

IF YOU DECIDE TO 'HIRE' TORONTO'S REAL ESTATE TEAM – THOMAS COOK & PARTNERS

First of all, we would be honoured! But more than that, we will provide you with our soft-cover condo seller book entitled 'Insider Tips For Getting The Best Price'.

Among other things, this informative guide is packed with valuable tips for making your home more saleable — tips that won't break the bank, either!

It also contains details about how Buyer Agency has changed the face of Toronto's real estate market and much, much more.

We also keep a list of 'Preferred Professionals,' from lawyers, to movers, to painters, to handymen, who come highly recommended by our clients. We would be happy to share their names with you so that you can rest assured that you won't be 'taken in' by shady operators.

This guide is available via mail OR by email as a PDF… tell us how you would like to receive it!

We Look Forward To Becoming YOUR Real Estate Consultants For Life!'

Since 1980, we have inspected thousands of homes and have advised many sellers about inexpensive — and mainly cosmetic — fix-up suggestions that have invariably improved the value of their homes.

Our Listing Specialists Will Do A Free, No-Obligation Room-By-Room Review Of Your Home!

If you're thinking of listing your home next week, next month, or even next year, it is never too soon to begin considering how to easily and inexpensively improve your home's appeal to buyers — and to maximize its value!

Sometimes, all it takes is some furniture rearranging!

But more often, some cosmetic improvements will help a lot, such as a fresh coat of paint.

SELLER HOMEWORK - 'IF YOU WERE THE BUYER...'

While You've Owned This Suite, What Have You Enjoyed The Most...

Breakthrough Marketing Program

What Will You Miss The Most...

Imagine you were the buyer looking at this home

Tell us the top 8 things you'll miss about living at this address - be very detailed

Before you answer this question, get a cup of tea or coffee and sit down in your favourite chair. Think about all the things that you've enjoyed while living in your home. We'd like to get your new buyer excited about those same things!

1.
2.
3.
4.
5.
6.
7.
8.

The point is to make someone else picture themselves living in your home. We will use these insights to help us prepare your feature sheet and web marketing!

LivingInToronto.com
Sell Your Home For The Best Price

Toronto's Real Estate Team - Thomas Cook and Partners, Sales Reps at RE/MAX Hallmark Realty Ltd., Brokerage 416-465-7850 Thomas@LivingInToronto.com

Breakthrough Marketing Program
Listing Information

Property Address: _____

Please assemble the following information to help us prepare our feature sheet and listing documents…

FOR CONDOS

- Realty tax bill for last / current tax year $ _____
- Electrical bill (total $) for last 12 months _____
- Annual condo insurance bill $ _____

- Latest year-end mortgage statement(s) from lender(s) (showing mortgage number, the current outstanding balance, your interest rate and its maturity date)
- Builder floor plans
- Copy of ALL door keys and fob (for condo building/elevator access)

- Order immediately a Status Certificate for your suite from your condo management office (cost is between $100 and $150 - depending on whether you get it from the management office or one of the online status certificate providers). Having this in our hands right away will prevent you from having your condo off the market for up to 10 banking days for a buyer's 'Conditional upon examination of Status Certificate' clause
- Parking space number _____ and Locker number _____
- Monthly condo maintenance payment $_____
- Condo fees include _____

FOR TENANTED PROPERTIES

- All Tenant personal information (names, phone numbers, hours at work, etc.)

Toronto's Real Estate Team - Thomas Cook and Partners. Sales Reps at RE/MAX Hallmark Realty Ltd., Brokerage 416-465-7850 Thomas@LivingInToronto.com

Are You Getting Your Money's Worth From Your Real Estate Agent?

Following are some key questions to ask when interviewing Realtors, followed by answers which apply to us… Toronto's Real Estate Team.

23 GREAT QUESTIONS TO ASK A REALTOR BEFORE SIGNING ANY LISTING AGREEMENT

1. **What guarantees do you offer me?**
    We guarantee that you'll be able to access feedback 24-7 from agents who have shown your home—provided they give it to us. We also guarantee in writing with our Easy Exit Listing Guarantee that if you aren't satisfied with our level of service to you, you can cancel your listing anytime.

2. **Really? Can we cancel the listing at any time WITH NO QUESTIONS ASKED, if we are unhappy?**
    People think "That's normal… every agent would do that" but it's NOT. We've had personal experience where the agent would not cancel the listing, even though no further showings were allowed!

    It's one of our guarantees and we mean it — no hassles, no strings attached, no questions asked. Period.

3. **I realize that automatically, through the efforts of the Toronto Real Estate Board, my home will be posted on the national website Realtor.ca and the Toronto MLS system with one or more pictures. Are you going to be posting additional digital pictures along with a detailed description about my home?**
    As a matter of course, we augment all our Realtor.ca listings with as many colour photos as we have available, a catchy headline and a detailed, professionally written description. We also use the 'Virtual Tour' link to post a Gallery of all our home photos… usually numbering up to 20 or more so the buyer has an excellent opportunity to get excited about your home.

4. **Do you have a website and will you post webpages about my home on the Internet? If so, what is the URL of your website?**
    We will devote detailed webpages to your property on our award-winning, high traffic website, **LivingInToronto.com** to attract Toronto buyers. Thousands of unique visitors a month will peruse 15 to 20+ colour pictures of your home, along with a detailed description of your home's interior, an interactive Google map as well as a virtual tour and YouTube video of your home.

5. **How familiar are you with Buyer Agency… can you counsel me effectively when a buyer's agent brings us an offer?**
    Precisely because we have a team of Buyer Specialists who act as Buyer Agents, we are intimately familiar with all the ins and outs of Buyer Agency, a concept that was introduced in Canada January 1st, 1995. Thomas obtained his ABR Designation (Accredited Buyer Representative) 20+ years ago and our Buyer Specialists must obtain their ABR designation immediately upon joining our team!

6. **Will you market my property by direct mail or email to potential buyers?**
    Letters, emails and Just Listed postcards or flyers often will be sent to appropriate potential buyer groups in our online database and to hundreds of neighbours around your property. We now have an email database of prospective Toronto buyers totaling over 25,000+ prospective buyers

and growing by hundreds per month. We include a "story" about your listed home in our FYI Toronto newsletter along with a link back to the digital photos of your condo or house on our website!

7. **Will you be providing prospective buyers or their agents with a detailed 4-6 page full colour feature sheet that includes: a professionally written description of my home's interior and exterior features; multiple colour photographs; a computer-generated floor plan; details about schools and other local landmarks; and financing options?**
Absolutely! There's even more details about why this is so important later in this Seller Breakthrough Marketing Program booklet.

8. **Do you have a buyer-focused website and other online resources that attracts many thousands of unique visitors every month and that has hundreds of pages of buyer-specific information that will help them to purchase my home?**
By now, we're sure, you know that the answer is yes! While many agents have websites, most are small, "cookie-cutter" ones with canned stories about themselves and of little value to home buyers. We are proud that we built our extensive website, **LivingInToronto.com**, from the ground up and that we update it OURSELVES constantly with timely, informative articles of interest to home buyers.

That way, prospective buyers return weekly to continue their home-buying education and to keep up with what's happening in the Toronto housing market. **We also take advantage of the tremendous market share RE/MAX has in Toronto—37% now and growing every year—to leverage your home's exposure to the home buying public.**

Your listing will also be displayed on several RE/MAX websites with broad exposure to many possible buyer markets—**TorontoHomesAndCondos.com** (locally), **Remax.ca** (nationally), **Remax.com** (North America) and internationally at **Global.Remax.com**—We do have international buyers coming to live and work in Toronto and you WANT your home easily available to them online!

9. **Do you have systems on your website that collect new email addresses daily of potential buyers for my home?**
You bet we do! Those email addresses go into our system and are given to us VOLUNTARILY by buyers impressed with our website AND who want more information about homes for sale in Toronto and the GTA.

10. **Do you automatically email your buyer prospect list the details of every new listing that you take?**
Yes, we do. And because people have given us their email addresses, they don't view the information that we send them about your home as unwanted "spam" to be discarded, unopened and unread.

11. **If you don't call or email me back within one business day of my contacting you, will you take $50 off the commission for each occurrence?**
Of course, we will! Yes, we're busy… busy serving valued clients just like you and answering your questions. That's our job! So, once your home's listed, we'll call you back right away. And because we don't have to spend all our time looking for new business, we spend a lot of our time doing what we should, which is keeping you informed and finding a buyer for your home.

12. **What systems do you have in place that will keep you in constant contact with me during the listing process and right through the transaction from offer acceptance to Celebration (closing) Day?**
We use a computerized checklist to monitor progress on the sale of your property up until the last two weeks. After that, a special "Last 10 Days" follow-up program begins… We will call often during the last 10 days prior to the closing date to ensure that everything is going smoothly, to answer any questions you may have and to solve any last-minute problems. We might even call your lawyer to see if we can offer him or her any assistance.

13. **Are you technologically up-to-date? Do you use landing pages to attract buyers—do you an email database to market your listings to—do you have an online follow-up system so you don't lose track of buyers who might be interested in your listings?**
Yes, yes, yes— and yes to the 'etc.' too! This may seem like a silly question, but we know agents who don't even have a computer or a client database let alone any other technology which allows us to have a 'High Tech—High Touch' business!

14. **Are you a full-time professional real estate consultant, or just a sales agent who works part-time?**
We are definitely full-time agents; Thomas has been licensed since 1980, and every buyer specialist on our Team is highly trained. We consider ourselves 'real estate consultants' who serve the needs of our 'Clients For Life' rather than as typical salespeople who view clients as just another commission. Our RE/MAX Team has won top awards from RE/MAX in Canada several times since 2000! **We have now helped over 2500 singles and families fulfill their real estate dreams.**

15. **What ongoing education have you enrolled in during the past 12 months to improve your level of service to clients?**
Thomas and our team members attend many seminars and webinars all throughout the year. At all these seminars, and during weekly teleconferencing calls, our Team members exchange information with Realtors from throughout North America and with expert marketers and real estate consultants. We firmly believe in being "cutting-edge" and recognize the importance of staying abreast of the ongoing technological revolution so that we can provide our clients with the very latest in effective marketing techniques.

16. **What expertise do you want your Realtor to have?**
Helping over 2500 buyers and sellers gives us lots of time "in the trenches" honing our negotiating and client-service skills. Let's do some more math… There are about 52,000+ agents in the Toronto Board. Last year TREB reported 92,000+ resales. That averages out to 1.8 sales per agent. Now we know that many of those 52,000+ licensed agents are in the business part-time, or on a casual basis. **But is that who you want to represent you when you sell your home?** Think of it this way: would you want a part-time surgeon to operate on you? Let's be generous and say that the average good active agent does 10-15 transactions a year… Given that figure, our team members still get 15-20 times the opportunity to learn, to gain experience and to stay sharp.

17. **How do you rank among your agent peers… are you one of your company's top Realtors?**
Thomas has his Certified Luxury Home Marketing Specialist designation and his ABR (Accredited Buyer Representative) designations. Thomas is a long-time member of the RE/MAX Circle of Legends. He has his RRS (Registered Relocation Specialist) and SRES (Retirement Real

Estate Specialist) designations. Thomas Cook has been in the Top 100 for RE/MAX in Canada and internationally several times in the two decades. And why? Because our team members make every one of our clients feel like they are our ONLY client!

18. **How much of your business is from past customers or referrals?**
    In any given year, it's 50+ per cent. We truly rely on referrals so we HAVE to provide such incredible, top-notch service that our clients are compelled to recommend us. Without those valuable recommendations, we could lose a significant portion of our business! That is quite a motivation in itself to "set the standard" among Toronto Realtors.

19. **How educated are you about negotiating?**
    After being in the business since 1980 and with our Team representing almost 2,500 families over the years, our Team Listing and Buyer Specialists have accumulated a lot of experience! We've got lots of great examples of how, by knowing exactly how the system works and its limitations, we have gained several extra thousands of dollars for our sellers.

20. **My equity is very important to me. Are you going to be tenacious in dealings with others on my behalf?**
    Most definitely! Thomas fights on your behalf as if it was his own home that he was selling! What's more… he enjoys being tenacious!

21. **How familiar are you with mortgage financing? Will you be able to personally advise me about the probability of the purchaser qualifying for a mortgage? Can you help the selling agent get financing for the buyer?**
    Thomas is very knowledgeable about financing and has been a licensed mortgage broker. He has often helped his buyers — and those of other agents — to get financing to buy their listings.

22. **How can I see what your clients are saying about you to verify your capabilities?**
    Easy—go online to **WhatPeopleAreSayingAboutUs.com** and watch 3rd-party video interviews with several clients.

23. **If I need it, how will you assist me in my relocation plans?**
    If you are relocating from anywhere in the world, we have a network of agents who work with the same By Referral Only mentality. Whether it's a community in Southern Ontario or anywhere else in Canada, the United States, or even worldwide, we can also refer you to like-minded RE/MAX agents. The benefit to you… is that you will be helped by someone who is interested in serving your needs first.

WE PROGRESS ALONG WITH TECHNOLOGY…

Since we're receiving 30-60+ email addresses monthly from new Toronto buyers (from several sources including our multiple websites) and we have an existing 25,000+ database of 'real estate interested' folks, it is important to communicate with these potential buyers and sellers with an educational email communications program.

We do several things to add value to this relationship that we're building on-line.'

First, we send a monthly FYI newsletter with informative buyer articles that help inform and teach purchasers more about the home-buying process and the housing market in Toronto.

Second, we include a few short, concise paragraphs with information about each of our new listings.

We do this in a conversational style by telling our readers some personal touches about our seller and complement that with specific house details and links back to the full-colour photos, video, Google map and property description that is posted on our Team website.

We've had some great response to this type of format (a request for 7 showings the first time we tried it) and our email buyer list is continuing to grow daily.

Finally, we have assembled an email list for the most active Realtors in Toronto.

Once we've listed a new house or condo, we email these agents with a short description of the home and a website link so they can look at the photos and video for themselves and, hopefully, show their buyer right away!

BREAKTHROUGH MARKETING PROGRAM

Service You SHOULD Get When Selling	What Most Agents Do	Our Team 'NO FRILLS' Basic Discounted Service	BREAKTHROUGH MARKETING With Guarantees
Prepare a Market Evaluation	Yes	Absolutely	Absolutely, with all the latest SOLDS
Get Free Advice About Cosmetic Fix-Ups That Add Value	Maybe	Absolutely	Absolutely
List Property On The Toronto Multiple Listing Service	Yes, with few or poorly taken photos	Absolutely, with SIX photos	Absolutely, with lots of photos and a professionally written description
Use PPPN Principles To Market Your Home		Absolutely	Absolutely
Provide Listing Guarantees		Absolutely	Absolutely
Expert Negotiation Of All Offers	Maybe	Absolutely, backed up by 37+ years of experience	Absolutely, backed up by 37+ years of experience
24/7 Agent Showing Feedback Reports			Absolutely, or you get $50 for every missed communication
Lockbox Security For Agent Access	Usually	Absolutely	Absolutely
Provide Full-Colour 4-6 Page Feature Sheets			Absolutely, with lots of colour photos & compelling condo description
Handling Of All Condo Showings	Yes	Absolutely	Absolutely
Create Online Listing Devoted To Your Property			Absolutely
Marketing On Facebook With A Boosted Post			Absolutely
Post Ads For Your Condo On Craigslist And/Or Kijiji			Absolutely
Email Broadcast To 25,000+ Potential Buyers			Absolutely
Showcase Your Condo On Affiliated RE/MAX Websites With Global Reach		Absolutely	Absolutely
Commission Rate Charged	3.5% - 6.0%	4.35%	5.0%

Sell fast, no hurry, need the maximum dollars to move up, corporate transfer, estate sale, stress free and more.

Because Every Seller Has Different Needs...

We've Designed One "NO FRILLS" And One Breakthrough Marketing Listing Plan For Our Clients That Maximize The Four PPPN Principles...

Since some sellers wish to have the option to hire a Realtor at a less expensive rate, we've designed our 'NO Frills' Discounted Commission Program!

While there sometimes is a perception that there is NO difference between agents and their marketing programs, nothing could be further from the truth.

Most agents don't provide more than the basic service and that's how the 'NO frills' discounted brokers make their pitch seem attractive.

If a seller wishes to have that type of service, we'll match it as follows for a reduced commission...

Our Basic 'NO Frills' Discounted Program

 We provide a complete 'on paper' market evaluation for your home… YOU determine what the true market value should be

 Cosmetic appeal is very important to the clear majority of buyers… we'll advise you with our Room-By-Room Review what inexpensive cosmetic improvements you should make to maximize your selling price

 Proper marketing and promotion of your home (once we've got Pricing and Presentation in place) will add thousands to your sale price and ensure it sells faster

 Full MLS exposure for your house or condo and uploaded to the public Realtor.ca site

 Expert negotiation of all offers (38+ years of expertise and experience!) … this alone puts us ahead of 99.5% of other Realtors

 Handling of all home showings by the RE/MAX Hallmark Realty Ltd Brokerage office

 Bi-weekly summaries of showing agent feedback (via email or voice) about market activity and showing results for your property and a review of your pricing after we do our 17-21-day market test and your property hasn't sold

 Lockbox security for agent access

 For every successful sale, we donate a portion of our income to help support the Children's Miracle Network and the Toronto Sick Kids Hospital

 Several full colour photos of your home posted to our affiliated RE/MAX real estate sites **TorontoHomesAndCondos.com**, **REMAX.ca**, **REMAX.com** and **Global.REMAX.com**

Our Breakthrough Marketing Program WITH Guarantees

Our Breakthrough Marketing Program includes the 'NO Frills' services PLUS all of the following…

 Full MLS exposure with up to 20 colour photos

 Online marketing focused on the ideal buyer demographic with an interactive virtual tour built into the property floor plan – see exactly what the view of each room is from multiple points

 Your own property webpage on our high-traffic **LivingInToronto.com** website… we upload lots of full colour digital photos and descriptive text to generate buyer excitement plus floor plans and a cash flow chart showing the buyer what his/her costs will be.

 Custom colour 4-6 page card-stock feature sheets that include digital camera interior and exterior photos, neighbourhood features, floor plans and condominium amenities

 Weekly ads on Craigslist or Kijiji online

 Email broadcast of your website photos and listing details to area real estate agents AND to our 25,000+ email database of 'real estate interested' people

 We may hire a professional home stager to come in and advise you on what to do to maximize your sale price

 'Boosted Post' ads on Facebook promoting your condominium aimed at your ideal buyer demographic

 Twice-a-week showings feedback report – find out what the buyers agents and their buyers are saying about your home and a review of your pricing after we do our 17-21-day market test and your property hasn't sold

 On occasion we'll put out special 'ugly' yellow signs in front of your condo building and in the neighbourhood (they increase the exposure and awareness of your home's listing by up to 700%)

 We can offer to negotiate discounted financing and provide lower down payment options for your home's buyer as an incentive for them to purchase YOUR property.

Here's What's Included In Our Powerful 4-6 Page COLOUR Feature Sheet!

 A layout that includes a minimum of 14 colour pictures of your home (ask Thomas to show you samples)

 A spreadsheet that gives a potential buyer the carrying costs for your home, depending upon the down payment, along with the income required to cover those costs — buyers have told us that they find this data extremely valuable

 A professionally written description of your home pointing out layout options, specific home features and other neighbourhood / condo building points of interest that buyers may not notice on their own.

WE GUARANTEE THAT YOU WILL SELL YOUR HOME FOR THOUSANDS MORE

IF You Follow Our Fix-Up Suggestions…

Avoid Giving The Buyer Thousands Of Your Dollars!

Call or text me today at 647-962-1650 to set up your free **Room-By-Room Review**.

If you would like to read more information about how best to prepare your home for sale, go to **RoomByRoomReview.com**.

You will read about the many valuable benefits of a pre-listing Room-By-Room Review!

This important pre-listing Room-By-Room Review is completely free and without any obligation.

We'll Pay You $500 On Closing!

If you don't believe that you got a higher price for your home after you completed all of the improvements that we suggest, we will credit you with $500 on closing. It's entirely your call!

Thomas Cook
Real Estate Sales Representative @ RE/MAX Hallmark Realty Ltd Brokerage

Mobile | 647-962-1650
Office | 416-465-7850

Web | LivingInToronto.com
Email | Thomas@LivingInToronto.com

Thomas Cook – Real Estate Sales Representative at
RE/MAX Hallmark Realty Ltd Brokerage

Author | Ultimate Toronto Home Buyer's Guide (THE 'Bible' for TO buyers)
Author | Toronto Home Buyer's Financing Guide
Author | Free Government Money Report (For 1st-time buyers)
Author | Insider Tips For Getting The Best Price (For condo sellers)
Author | Guide To Attracting The Best Tenants
Author | Best Capital Gains Tax Advice (Excellent investor advice)
Author | Guide To Downtown Toronto Condo Prices
Author | Insider Advice For House Sellers (For house sellers)

ARE YOU ALSO A TORONTO CONDO OR HOUSE BUYER?

If you are, you might benefit greatly from reading one or more of these books too

Get a clear understanding about everything you need to know when buying a Toronto condo or house

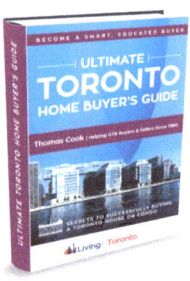

Free download for Toronto buyers at…
UltimateHomeBuyersGuide.com

Avoid costly mistakes when getting pre-approved for a mortgage

Get your mortgage financing questions answered at…
HomeBuyersFinancingGuide.com

Learn how to sell your Toronto house

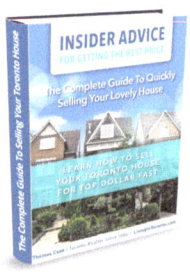

Solid advice for HOUSE sellers at…
InsiderAdviceForHouseSellers.com

Get free money from the federal government

Free download for 1st-time buyers at…
FreeGovernmentMoneyReport.com

CHAPTER TITLES FROM OUR 'INSIDER TIPS FOR GETTING THE BEST PRICE' BOOK

Here's the chapters list from our book designed to help Toronto condominium owners get the absolute best price for their home.

Take a look and pick which chapters it might benefit you to read right away.

1	Home Seller Timeline Explained	1
2	Beware Of Awkward Sensory Experiences Destroying Your Sale	3
3	Being Beautiful Matters No Matter The Size	6
4	3 Improvements Not To Do Before Selling Your Condo	9
5	A Free Service - Get A Room-By-Room Review Done	12
6	Bright Ideas For Making Successful Lighting Choices	15
7	Successful Ways To Avoid Dreadful Scarcity Thinking	17
8	Be Fearless When Making Perfect Colour Choices	19
9	Pay The Highest Attention To This Important Room	21
10	Ensure You Answer These 4 Not-So-Surprising Buyer Questions	24
11	11 Surefire Ways To Get Your Condo Ready For Sale	27
12	Creating An Effective Buyer Profile For Your Awesome Condo Suite	30
13	9 Downsizing Tips To De-Clutter And De-Stress Your Move	33
14	If You Were The Interested Buyer…	35
15	How To Avoid An Upcoming Showing Meltdown	37
16	5 Best Ways To Absolutely Ensure Your Tenanted Condo Suite Sells	40
17	Know You Want To Sell But Dread All Those Showings?	45
18	How To Make Awesome Decisions When Selling And Buying Together	47
19	Great Advice When Closing Dates Don't Match	50
20	Get Ready… Showings Start Tomorrow At 10 am	53
21	Today's Market Realities - Selling In A Seller's Market	57
22	Find Out How Much Your Toronto Condominium Is Worth	60
23	Not Sure How To Price Your Home? Avoid Mistakes With These Tips	63
24	Who Represents You In A Real Estate Transaction?	67
25	So How Do Real Estate Agents Get Paid?	70
26	You'll Be Asked To Sign A Listing Agreement	72
27	Once The Listing Agreement Is Signed, Now What?	75
28	Critical… Order The Condominium Status Certificate Immediately	76
29	We Might See These Typical Clauses In Any Condo Offer	78
30	What Happens At The Offer Presentation?	82
31	5 Things You Need To Ask Yourself Before Turning Down A Low-Ball Offer	86
32	Why Seller's Remorse Is So Common, And What To Do About It	89
33	How The Closing Process Works - A Checklist Of The Critical Steps	92
34	Planning A Stress-Free Move	95
35	Closing Costs For The Condo Seller	98
36	Choosing The Right Professional Is Not Easy	101
	To Summarize…	102
	Here's The Free Stuff You Can Get From Us	104
	Appendix	111
	Plain English Version Listing Documents	
	You Absolutely, Positively Need To Know What These Mean	
	Real Estate Terms You Should Know	
	Mortgage Terms You Should Know	

NOTES

www.ingramcontent.com/pod-product-compliance
Lightning Source LLC
Chambersburg PA
CBHW051055180526
45172CB00002B/648